Effective leadership styles for managers

ALPHA-X

Charith Venkat Pidikiti

February 2019

Author

Charith is a 1986 born, globetrotter and a biomedical engineer, who currently lives in Munich, Germany. A true jack-of-all-trades who religiously follows four words, "Ambition has no limits". Apart from being a full time employee at a Fortune 500 company, he is also an entrepreneur, an artist, a drummer, a fitness aficionado and a writer, who loves and collects classic cars and history books.

Hailing from India, a country rich in diverse religions and varied cultures, he was always obsessed with history, mythology and religion, yet it was his penchant for science since a young age that led him to study at the New York University, in one of the largest cosmopolitan cities of the world, NYC. After which he moved to work in Germany, where he is currently working on his Doctorate, has accomplished over four medical and two business publications and won the "Making A Difference" Award.

He constantly travels around the world with curiosity, learning foreign traditions, cultures, religions, modern technology or simply in pursuit of new experiences.

Follow the Author:

https://instagram.com/charithvenkat

https://www.facebook.com/charith.venkat

Copyright © Charith Venkat Pidikiti 2018

All rights reserved

Charith Venkat Pidikiti asserts the moral right to be identified as the author of this work.

Although the author and publisher have made every effort to ensure that the information in this book was correct at press time, the author and publisher do not assume and hereby disclaim any liability to any party for any loss, damage, or disruption caused by errors or omissions, whether such errors or omissions result from negligence, accident, or any other cause.

ISBN: 9781090564283

Cover concept and Design by Alpha-X

ANNOTATION

This book deals with the general principles or managers and their various leadership styles out of which key effective styles are described in more detail along with a reasoning for why and how they are effective. The book also gives a description of general terms used within.

KEY WORDS

- Charismatic
- Interactional
- Laissez-faire
- Lead
- Leader
- Leadership
- Management
- Manager
- Servant
- Transactional
- Transformational

TABLE OF CONTENTS

1. INTRODUCTION..7
2. MANAGER...7
3. LEADERSHIP..9
    3.1 Leadership types..5
    3.2 Leadership Styles...7
4. CONCLUSIONS...31
5. BIBLIOGRAPHY AND WEB RESOURCES...................34

INTRODUCTION

Any project, department or team irrespective of its size or number needs someone to guide or lead it. This could be a person appointed specifically for this purpose, a person within the team or even a group of two or more people internal or external to the project, work, or team that is managed. Successful managers show certain traits of leadership skills and styles which they have acquired through experience, mentorship, intercultural exchanges, enterprise environmental factors, or simply innate to the person etc. These various styles can be very different from each other with varying effects. Managers may have experience with multiple styles but often have to choose the style most appropriate for the work planned, the team, and the general environment they are working in, such as the place, country, its culture etc.

MANAGER

A manager is generally a person who is assigned to lead a group of people responsible for achieving a certain task, project or work. In his role, he mentors, administers manages and controls the group or resources towards the collective goal. The group that is being led can be his peers or subordinates but sometimes even his superiors depending on the situation he is appointed in. Roles in an organization that could be considered as managers are, supervisor, administrator, head of the department, director, managing director, employer, superintendent, organizer etc. The manager's roles, responsibilities, relationships and leadership can be highly influenced by the organizational structure and governance.

Successful managers generally possess the following attributes:

- Knowledge about the work or project that is being managed
- Specific technical tools and expertise
- Adept to problem solving
- Leadership skills needed to manage, collaborate, motivate, direct and coordinate work with a team
- Effective communication
- The right personality, aptitude, ethics and attitude
- Managing conflict
- Drive others to achieve their own success

LEADERSHIP

Successful completion of a group task require leaders with good skills. Leadership is the ability to lead a team and inspire them to do their jobs well. Leadership is necessary from the very beginning of any activity to its very end. There is a wide range of leadership theories and styles available, but it is the responsibility of the leader or manager to pick and use as needed for each situation or team. It is of utmost importance for the manager to communicate and express the vision and also to inspire and encourage the team to achieve the desired outcome[1]. Furthermore, it is the manager's responsibility to assess the caliber, ability and willingness of the team to perform their tasks or work, in order to adapt their leadership and management styles. For example, novice or in-experienced team members with lower skills might require more assistance and training than the ones with higher ability and experience. Occasionally the manager might decide to use more than one type of skill within the same team depending on the situation. Through effective leadership, the manager can get the commitment required from his team.

---

[1] PMI – A Guide to the Project Management Body of Knowledge, sixth edition, September 6, 2017, Page 350

Leadership types

There are several ways to lead and several kinds of leaders. Not all of the methods are optimal in all situations. Oftentimes, managers must learn to fit into the organization and their leadership style is influenced by the leadership type they practice in, either from the top down or from the bottom up. Examining the pros and cons of these two disparate methods can help one determine what kind of leader a managers wants to be, in order to make the maximum positive impact on the organization.

Following are the different leadership types:
Top down: This is the most typical type of leadership in most organizations around the world, where a person or manager in a superior role is directing or leading a team reporting to him from a subordinate level. The manager in this case also works with other managers within the organization who are also reporting to him, to ensure they are directing their individual teams in a desired fashion, telling them what do to and when to do them in a chain of command. The manager also spends time with his own leaders and superiors within the organization getting direction from them and passing it down the chain.

The primary benefit in this sort of arrangement is that the managers have a high level of visibility sometimes even in detail. Employees in different levels, roles or job titles know who to approach in need of direction, assistance or delegation. For example, a customer service engineer would go to his supervisor in need of direction when he gets a call from an angry customer who is unsatisfied with the service. The supervisor in turn would either make the decision himself or approach his manager for a solution and finally pass that solution or direction down to the customer service engineer to apply that solution for the customer.

The biggest disadvantage in this arrestment is that the manager leading a team does not necessarily understand what is going on in the team or the challenges faced by them, as he is not in the trenches with the workers, hence the team may not always respect the leader. The relay of this information upwards regarding the challenges faced by his subordinates could also be hindered because of that. For example, a team working to meet a deadline has a big hurdle because of one of their contractors who fails to submit their part of the work. The team has informed the manager but the manager feels that the work can still be done as the team has enough members to complete the task. He relays the message to his superiors but gets back the response to stick to the dead line no matter what, so he in turn pushes his team to do so.

Bottom up: A manager working in a bottom up leadership type generally spends most of his time at the workers level, working alongside his subordinates, trying to understand the various challenges they face by experiencing them first hand. This is generally accomplished when he takes on the same level tasks or a portion of the tasks to be up close and personal with the working environment, the problems, the work itself that is being performed etc. The manager is leading his team upwards from being in the trenches with them and they do not push all the work and direction from his own superiors downward onto the workers but rather helps them determine which tasks needs to be done, in what priority, what resources are required and in which methodology to follow. For example, the managers understands why the coding cannot be completed by the deadline as he is working side by side with his team and knows that they don't have the needed software promised by their contractors. Although he gets pressure from his own superiors to stick to the dead line, he is in a much better positon to explain to the superior why his team are unable to comply.

The primary advantage in this arrangement is that the managers has the perspective, which someone from a top down type of leadership will not have. He gets the respect and the traction from his resources as they feel a sense of connection to him.

Leadership styles

Managers can lead their teams in multiple ways. The style chosen by the manager can be a personal preference or a result of multiple factors associated with the work or project. The chosen style can change depending on several factors, such as time or duration changes, team changes, work environment changes or political changes to name a few. Some of the major factors to consider include but not limited to:

- Characteristics of the environment such as economic state or social situation
- Characteristics of the leader such as moods, values, ethics, attitudes
- Characteristics of the organization such as its structure, its work and purpose
- Characteristics of the team members such as their needs, attitudes, cultural background, experience or age

Some of the most common leadership styles based on research are:

Autocratic leadership: This style is characterized typically with one person who assumes the role of a "boss", who makes all the decisions and gives directions with little to no feedback from his or her subordinates or team members. Orders are generally pushed onto the team members irrespective of their agreement to the direction. In other words, the leader does not consult subordinates prior to making a decision. They make the decision first and then communicate them to the team, expecting them to comply and promptly implement the decision. There is little or almost no flexibility in the work and schedule in this type of environment. Communication is generally only active downward towards resources and rarely upward towards managers.

The Autocratic leader makes all the policies, procedures, work instructions and guidelines that he expects the team to follow and execute indefinitely. There is no research to support this style of leadership as being truly successful in the modern society. Examples of leaders that follow this style of leadership include Donald Trump from the Trump organization and Albert J Dunlap from Sunbeam Corporation among others.

Democratic leadership: This style is centered on the subordinates' or the team's contributions. Unlike the autocratic leadership style, the democratic leadership style involves the team in making decisions and collecting feedback from them before executing the directed work. Although the democratic manager holds the final responsibility, he or she delegates the authority to team members who make decisions regarding the work projects.

Communication in this style of leadership is generally active both upwards towards managers and downwards towards subordinates. Feedback is collected both ways and acted upon leading to continuous improvement in terms of the work performed and scheduling. A lessons learned register is also maintained as part of the organizational process assets which contains all the feedback, conflict resolutions, methods which worked and those that did not etc. Often entailing competence, fairness, intelligence, courage, honesty and creativity, this style of democratic leadership is one of the most preferred and successful leadership within an organization.

Strategic leadership: This style is often centered on a manager I a high leading position or in the upper level management, such as the head of the organization, however the strategic leadership style is not limited to only those at the top of the organization. A strategic leader forms the liaison between the need for new solutions, opportunities and a need for practicality by displaying good judgment decisions. The manager spends more half his time and resources towards strategic thinking to deliver the right products for the organization.

In other words, the managers strategically leads his team depending on the capabilities and motivation levels of the team to ensure both the team and the organization come out equally satisfied.

Transformational leadership: This style of leadership uses idealized behaviors and values, strong vision, high aspirations, idealized characteristics, introspection, inspirational motivation, encouraging innovation and creativity, and considering each team members individually to empower the team to their best. This style is about bringing a transformation or initiating a change in the team members, the organization and others. Managers generally motivate not only their team members but also their peers to do more than intended and often end up achieving more than planned. They sought out new challenges and innovation for themselves and their teams, which is necessary to survive competition. Transformational leadership brings in new ideas to the organizations products to drive change and to grow. This is very important to continuously manage resources as time and business demands change and evolve.

Transformational leaders provide their followers with new opportunities, which in turn makes them more satisfied and committed towards them. A good transformational leader having strong and clear vision can lead individuals and groups to sustainable and successful development by bringing in continuous change through which the team members not only connect well with the leader but also adopt integrity and accountability. A good example would be a nonprofit organization, where the members work above their self-interest, creating a sense of trust among individuals, which enables them to connect well with each other and with the manager. Ideally, this style crates change agents in the system who in turn inspire others.

Team Leadership: This style of leadership involved the creation of a roadmap for a rough prediction of the future (often positive) in order to not only provide a direction but also to give a sense of purpose, which in turn gives the team inspiration by means of the strong vision. For example, a manager shares his vision with the team, that within six months, they will have higher budget projects that will in turn bring in more stakeholders who invest more into the company and therefore more challenging work and new experiences.

Team leadership involves working with not only the minds of the team members but also their hearts, to identify what each person wants and to sketch a roadmap that ensures everyone gets what they desire, even if it is only partly. Team leadership recognizes that teamwork might not always involve relationships that are cooperative and trusting. Whether or not the plan and the team will succeed is the most challenging aspect of this style of leadership and it may fail due to poor leadership qualities of the manager[2].

There are seven pillars of team leadership according to Jan Makela, an executive coach, speaker and best-selling author of "Cracking the Code to Success and Be the Manager People Won't Leave", which are as follows[3]:

1. Vision and Mission
2. Goals
3. Expectations
4. Feedback
5. Treat everyone fairly but not equal
6. Provide tools and resources to do quality work
7. Celebrate success

---

[2] Why Teams Don't Work, Diane Coutu, *Harvard Business Review* MAY 2009 ISSUE

[3] Cracking the Code to Success and Be the Manager People Won't Leave, Jan Makela, 2012

Cross-Cultural Leadership: This style of leadership typically exists in environments with multiple cultures or a society with various cultures. Communication is a big challenge in this style and hence also of upmost importance here as having multiple cultures and background of the team members could easily lead to misunderstandings. The Manager has to be sensitive, empathic and knowledgeable of the cultures and their traditions etc. Intercultural gaps (Components such as enterprise, jobs, national generational cultures) can threaten any project and lead to clashes and failure. Managers should have the ability to not only manage these gaps but also to leverage and through that even enhance their leadership skills at both a personal and at a team level.

In a contemporary global market, the front runners are often recognized through this style of leadership. For example, car manufacturers Toyota and BMW have been jointly developing the „Supra" set to release in 2019, however due to many cultural as well as language gaps, they faced a lot of challenges that ultimately lead to delays and quality issues. Finally it was Masayuki Kai San who bridged this gap and got both teams from Germany and Japan to iron out the differences and come to an agreement in their car's design, quality etc. This could only be accomplished because Masayuki Kai San lived in Germany for several years before moving back to Japan where he originally is from, so he is well versed in both the cultures, etiquette, and languages[4].

Managers working in international organization practicing this style of leadership often have to identify and actively manage the intercultural factors within their environment, adjust their leadership proactively and suggest practical ways for the same to others in order for it to work with the different cultures.

Facilitative Leadership: This style of leadership focuses mainly on outcomes, performance, measurement and scores rather than on the skills of the teams. the efficacy of its process is directly related to the effectiveness of a team and it takes much skill to master any task. A manager exercising this style uses a light hand on the process as a facilitative leader if the team is high performing, but the same manager will employ strong directives in aiding the team to function if the team is low performing, by mentoring, guiding, monitoring group dynamics, process improvement suggestions, interventions or training to keep the team on track and towards a common goal.

Laissez-faire Leadership: This style involves encouraging the subordinates to establish their own goals and make their own decisions by giving them authority, in other words this

---

[4] https://www.kleinezeitung.at/wirtschaft/4985240/Auftrag-fuer-Graz_Magna_Im-Windschatten-von-BMW-rollt-Toyota-an

style can also be known as taking a hands-off style. The teams or departments are given the authority to work according to their own liking with very little to no interference of the manager according to Angelo Kinicki from AZcentral[5]. Contradictory to what it may sound like, according to research this style of leadership has been discovered to be the least effective style of management and also least satisfactory for the teams since there is often disagreements amongst team members who do not have a common directive from superior.

For example, senior managers of a smartphone company have decided to follow Laissez-faire Leadership and have given their teams full authority to makes their own decisions and designs for their smartphone and also the contents such as hardware, apps etc. Unfortunately, the teams could not come to a common agreement to put it together and ended up making a device that had too many things and was not at all user friendly. Ultimately, the managers had to take over and pick only a few features from the brain storming session and user feedback and give common directives and strict instructions to their teams. This has led to a lot of time and resource negative loss.

---

[5] https://eu.azcentral.com/story/money/business/career/2015/07/06/hands-off-leader-can-derail-employees/29798273/

Transactional Leadership: This style of leadership is also called "management by exception", where rewards are determined based on goals, target accomplishment and feedback by maintaining the status quo. Transactional leadership style is a more traditional method used widely across different organizations and has been used since several years. The team members get tangible rewards immediately as individuals or as a group, for following the orders by the manager, which makes it sort of an exchange process. For example, the leader gives and order, the employee follows and executes the order, the leader verifies that the outcome is as he had expected/intended (or exceeded expectations) and rewards the employee for his or her performance. This style of leadership motivates the team members by appealing to their own self-interest as it also entails corrective actions to improve the workers' performance.

Overall, transactional leadership focuses on the exchange of work and rewards. The most important points necessary for the transaction are:

1. Giving clear orders/instructions/outcome expectations
2. Explaining how said expectations can be met
3. Tracking the progress with focus on objectives
4. Giving/taking continuous feedback

5. Awarding rewards which are contingent to meeting the expectations.

The downsides of transactional leadership style are:

1. That it not only awards top-performers but it also (in some cases) punishes low-performers
2. Managers applying this style are not often concerned about achieving change but rather about maintaining normal operations and conditions of the performing organization.

Coaching Leadership: This style focuses primarily on training, supervising or mentoring the subordinates. The manager teaching his subordinates is operational in influencing where the performance or results need continuous improvement. In other words, the team members are trained to become their best versions and enhance their skills, in any given field of activity or role. Through this kind of mentorship, the coaching manager ensures a high-level motivation, encouragement and the inspiration of his subordinates and even his peers.

Just like a successful sports coach, the coaching style manager should also follow these six strategies[6]:

---

[6] https://www.inc.com/articles/2001/04/22404.html

1. Have a clear vision and road map to ensure all the team members have the same focus on the outcome.

2. Associate the vision with individual goals. As Jamie Walters (Inc.com) suggests "A personal coach is only as effective as the client is motivated. A coach can recommend approaches and tools until she is blue in the face, but if the client isn't genuinely focused on attaining the expressed goals ... little change will be made."

3. Know individual strengths and weaknesses of the subordinates, and have a plan to minimize or remove those weaknesses

4. The right person for the right job. To place a team member in a role that matches his skills.

5. The right communication methods and content in order to coach the team member in a way that suits the person.

6. Celebrate upon achieving the set goals and targets.

Charismatic Leadership: This style of leadership is often practiced my managers who are highly enthusiastic, self-confident, energetic, holds strong convictions and is able to inspire others around them. This is a personality-based leadership and not all managers have the ability to lead in this manner, as the characteristics necessary for charismatic leadership are innate to the person itself. Oftentimes the manager exhibits his or her innovatory control. Charisma involves a transformation of the team members' beliefs and values and it does not just mean sheer change in their behaviour, which differentiates a charismatic leader from an ordinary general leader. Therefore, a charismatic leader is more prepared to transform his or her teams' underlying normative direction that structures specific attitudes.

Simply put, charismatic leadership is the method of inspiring certain behaviours in team members and peers by way of persuasion, force of personality and eloquent communication. Charismatic managers motivate their subordinates to improve the way certain things are done or simply to get things done.

A great example of a Charismatic leader is Martin Luther King Jr.

Visionary Leadership: This style involves managers who recognizes that people are the most important resource for all the steps, processes and methods of leadership. Almost all the successful managers who lead their teams towards the goal successfully have certain aspects of vision in them, however some of them stand out as being highly visionary and these managers are the ones considered as demonstrating this style of leadership. Creativity and discipline are very necessary for the right vision, which is in turn necessary for sustaining any project within an organization. The manager needs to have clear communication skills to propagate this vision to all his followers in order to achieve long-term goals.

A visionary manager is a focused leader who has the capability to motivate his team members to reach not only their individual goals but also the goals of the organization. He or she has the potential to see how the goal and the path to the goal should be and how to get there. Visionary managers are generally great change agents.

The three main characteristics of a visionary leader are[7]:

- They are risk takers.
- They are great listeners (feedback)
- They take responsibility

Servant-Leader Leadership: This type of leadership demonstrates commitment to serving and putting other people. It focuses on the team members' well-being, autonomy, learning, development and growth to which they belong. The manager exercising this style of leadership generally concentrates mainly on relationships, collaboration

---

[7] https://www.thebalancecareers.com/visionary-leadership-4174279

and community as a team and organization as a whole rather than leadership and authority, which only comes second and only emerges after service to others. Servant leadership is the way to empower the team, in order to enable the highest team performance. Servant leadership has reduced overall controlling of the subordinates by the manager. For example in an agile approach, the need for servant leadership more than the manager itself. In most modern practices and organizations (generally involving millennials), it is recommended that the manager develops a servant or cooperative leadership rather than maintain an autocratic leadership.

A Servant leader shares the authority and power, puts the requirements of his subordinates first and supports them in their growth and development in order to perform at their best. The manager may step in to do some of the work where he or she needs to but always keep in mind the well-being of the staff ahead of everything.

The downside is that it is difficult to be a Servant Leader if the manager is solely accountable for project success. In theory the development team all share ownership, but in reality if things go wrong then it is the manager that will face the consequences of failure, not them. This means that naturally the manager has an impetus to step in if things are going wrong and implement decisive corrective action, but as such then destroy the self-organizing nature of the team.

Interactional Leadership: This style of leadership comes from a combination of charismatic leadership, transformational leadership and transactional leadership. Managers who practice this style of leadership usually dedicate time to understand the interactions and relationships of his team to place himself or herself in the chain. Successful international leadership is determined by the relationship between the manager's personality and the specific situation. The interaction occurs when the behaviour of the manager e.g. Charismatic – Energetic, causes a change in the behaviour of his team members. This change itself is a response that stimulates the relationship.

Analytical Leadership: This style depends on the managers own technical knowledge and skills. Analytical managers generally make the technical decisions for the task, which they communicate to their teams. The teams then follows the decisions and execute them.

The three main qualities of an analytical leader are[8]:

- Awareness - environment and assumptions

---

[8] https://www.lebow.drexel.edu/news/three-qualities-of-analytical-leader

- Influence - effectively guide others to achieve desired goals

- Information sharing and collaboration – Amongst team members

Combined together, analytical leaders tactically combine awareness, influence, and collaboration to their advantage, so they can efficiently leverage the available information for reaching organizational goals.

CONCLUSIONS

Leadership is the ability to lead a team and inspire them to achieve high performance. A manager requires a wide range of leadership skills through all phases of the product life cycle. A manager can develop strong leadership skills by applying them creatively to communicate vision and inspire stakeholders to support the work and outcomes of the project. Managers make or break the organizations. It is said everything rises and falls on a manager's leadership. Everything! Not something, not a few things, which means everything rises and falls on leadership. One cannot lead a team if he or she is not up to date with best practices, current business environment or different cultures to name a few. If the world is transforming, managers need to work on themselves first before bringing a change in their subordinates. Unfortunately, most of the managers in today's world are like ticketing agents. They want to take their customers where they have never been. Managers are more of tour guides where they lead team systematically and show them instead of telling them, as people follow more of what they see rather than what they hear. The kind of leadership style should be tailored to the team that is to be managed. A leader needs to have a bag of styles to pull out to create their own custom style that will work well with the team. Good managers should use different hats of leadership as per requirement. One cannot be successful on a project by applying just one type of leadership style all the time, in every situation and with all the stakeholders. A great leader or manager always needs to consider his team's well-being and development, he needs to motivate and inspire his subordinates to follow him and at the same time consider the surroundings such are the organization and the general environment.

Apart from all the above the manager also needs to have the right personality traits such as, being authentic, courteous, creative, culturally sensitive, emotional intelligence, intellectual, service-oriented, socially responsible, systemic etc.

It is very important for a manager to be the right kind of leader for any team assigned to him or her, by choosing the right style, at the right time for any type of teams, with any kind of background but must always follow these steps in any type of leadership:

1. Continually evaluate the business environment and propose a vision.
2. Express this vision through persuasion and encouragement.
3. Gain the trust of those you want to share your vision and engage them in this vision.
4. Lead others in fulfilling this vision.

In order to unlock a style's true potential, the manager should be broadly accepted by all and it is up to the manager to use his strategy, experience and skills to gain that trust through leading my example. A successful manager leads by giving his subordinates, guidance, influence, collaboration using relational power, developing self, innovating ideas, focusing on relationships with people, inspiring trust, focusing on long-range vision, ask what and why instead of when and how, focusing on the horizon instead on the bottom line, challenging the status quo instead of accepting it, doing the right things at the right time instead of simply doing the things right, focusing on vision, alignment, motivation and inspiration.

BIBLIOGRAPHY AND WEB RESOURCES

- MTD Training Leadership Skills Ventus Publishing ApS 2010
- Personality Styles: We're all Different, Aren't We?, Crumb, Cheryl, C.E. Biz, May, 2005. http://www.ccrumb.com/articles/may05en.pdf
- The Leadership-Integrity Link Gen Ronald R. Fogleman, AU-24, Concepts for Air Force Leadership: http://www.au.af.mil/au/awc/awcgate/au-24/fogleman.pdf
- PMI – A Guide to the Project Management Body of Knowledge, sixth edition, September 6, 2017
- Why Teams Don't Work, Diane Coutu, Harvard Business Review MAY 2009 ISSUE

www.ingramcontent.com/pod-product-compliance
Lightning Source LLC
Chambersburg PA
CBHW021853170526
45157CB00006B/2421